POSITIVE VISION

ENJOYING THE ADVENTURES AND ADVANTAGES OF POOR EYESIGHT

KEN BRANDT

More info: KenBrandt.com

ISBN hardcover 978-0-6487625-2-2
Published by Ken Brandt
Biography, Adventure, Self-Help, Humor

Contents

Foreword

Rob Youl

From earliest days one of my favourite poems has been *On First Looking into Chapman's Homer,* by John Keats, which includes the lines:

**Then I felt like some watcher of the skies
When a new planet swims into his ken;**

'Ken', meaning 'awareness, knowledge, recognition' and in this context 'gaze', is highly apt, as my friend Ken Brandt has introduced me to a new planet. He has invited, indeed compelled me, to celebrate new dimensions of perception.

We met six years ago when he formed an early morning exercise group in our local park. It has led to robust physical activity, broader contacts in the neighbourhood, occasional social get-to-gethers and firm and supportive friendships. Ken's love of fitness permeates our activities.

I soon discovered Ken plays the trumpet in more than one jazz band, going all out to share the delights of his music, both on stage and in the streets.

For some years, however, little suggested to me that Ken had sight problems – after all he had travelled widely and had had a long career in management. His innate modesty meant that I only learned recently he had managed many multi-million dollar business projects, and had founded and led two Wall Street information technology and security consultancies.

So it was more than slightly surprising when in the park over planks and push-ups that he announced that he was writing a book on living with poor eyesight, appropriately and engagingly in the year 2020.

The volume before you reflects his cheerful toughness and capacity to meet challenges, his sensitivity, disarming humour, adventurous spirit, conviviality, industry and professionalism.

There is something here for everyone – but for lucky me, who late in life can still read, use computers and sketch without glasses, it's inspiring.

I like its spirit of self-help and the stories of his boyhood, his New York City bachelor days, his total lack of claustrophobia in the caverns of northeast America, his aerial daring as a skydiver, his affinity for his parents and brother. I envy him his times on the range in Montana, which remind me of my youthful adventures hitching across the lower 48.

I see him selling beer to bleachers packed with sports fans and sitting attentively in board meetings. He's in restaurants, socialising with charm and frankness at penthouse parties, and quietly but firmly exemplifying racial and cultural tolerance. Interestingly, he shows, as do all good writers, that we can see almost as well through words as with our eyes.

Thank you, Ken – and well done! A ripper[1] read!

> Rob Youl OAM RFD[2]
> Landcare worker, forester, sketcher, retiree, resident of South Melbourne, Victoria, Australia

---

1 Ripper: Australian slang for 'bewdy', 'bonzer', 'ribuck' or 'slashing'
2 Rob was awarded the OAM, which stands for Medal of the Order of Australia, for involvement in national community conservation programs; Rob received the Reserve Force Decoration (RFD) in recognition of his long service as an engineer officer in the Australian Army Reserve.

Chapter 1

Longer Life

> *"Nobody sees reality whole; we all need others to show us the parts of it that they see better than we do. Nobody sees reality with total accuracy; we all need others to correct our own vision."*
> *–Lewis B. Smedes*

A Few Things to Avoid for a Longer Life

I like going fast. Walking fast, running, sprinting, generally good. Bicycling and roller blading, fun, but not so good, because I can easily go faster than I can see the bumps and potholes coming up. Driving is really fun, but I don't see nearly well enough to get a license, which is a good thing for society. Skydiving sounded fast and fun, but I probably should have thought about being able to spot the landing area before trying it.

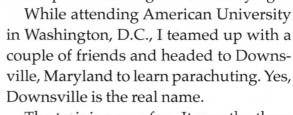

While attending American University in Washington, D.C., I teamed up with a couple of friends and headed to Downsville, Maryland to learn parachuting. Yes, Downsville is the real name.

The training was fun. It was the three of us along with another forty or so people we didn't know. We trained with old-school round parachutes, not the more modern rectangular sports variety. It was actual training, rather than purely an exciting thrill ride. We were not going on tandem jumps strapped to an experienced skydiver who controls the jump out of the plane, the dive, the parachute steering, and the landing. We weren't going to be connected to anyone. We were learning how to do everything on our own.

First, we learned how to land. This is also a valuable skill if you ever need to jump out of a relatively low window of a burning building. You may break your legs, but the rest of you should be OK. As you touch the ground, you absorb some landing pressure with your ankles and knees, then quickly roll onto your side, and then onto your back. It doesn't hurt at all if you do it right.

Skydiving hopefuls practice this landing roll four ways, to be ready no matter which way the wind takes them: front left, front right, back left, and back right. After getting good at it at ground level, you move up to jumping off a two-foot-high box, then one that is about six-feet high. Next step is taking the leap with eyes closed: As you near the ground, the instructor yells out which direction to roll. Practice gives you a nice sense of confidence.

Instructors provide helpful guidance on opening and steering the parachute, and how to deploy a spare if the primary one doesn't open. You also learn – but don't practice – what to do if you are about to hit a bunch of tree branches: Cross your legs!

We didn't have to open the primary parachute ourselves on the first three jumps because it was attached to the plane via a cord and designed to deploy automatically. However, knowing about the backup parachute comes in handy if something goes wrong.

Just thinking about my first jump pumped up my adrenaline. I got into a little plane with a seat for the pilot and just enough space on the floor to cram in an instructor and three or four skydivers. The plane had no door, just an opening. That's something I noticed right away when we took off, since I was sitting just inches from the opening where the door should be. We flew a bit, and all the while I was a little concerned about being so close to the wild blue yonder.

It was time. It was my turn. Using a tight grip, I climbed out through the opening and into position. I was now hanging on outside, facing forward as the plane continued to move. My feet were on a metal bar over one of the wheels, my hands holding onto a metal bar under one of the wings.

Once the plane was in position, the instructor – who was inside the plane – yelled "Jump!" At least that's what I think he said. I could only hear the full roar of the engine and the rushing wind.

After holding on with all my might, it was time to let go. I jumped backward and slightly up, and immediately started dropping, watching as the plane sped away.

It seemed like an eternity before my parachute opened. I spent those long moments wondering whether it was time to go for the backup plan I'd learned. Luckily, I didn't act on that thought, and my main parachute opened just fine.

It was beautiful.

I floated down, wishing the whole thing could go on longer. Figuring out where to land turned out to be fairly easy. I steered toward the only big field without crops, trees, or houses. When I got lower, I could see a lot of people in a circle on the field and headed for them. Getting even lower, I could see the Frisbee-size target in the middle of the circle, aimed for it, and came pretty close. It was a successful landing.

It was great! What could possibly go wrong? It didn't take

long for me to get a couple of examples, one minor, one major.

I wanted to jump again right away. They gave me the option of packing my parachute or using one someone else had already prepared. I wanted to learn everything about the sport, plus I thought I should be responsible for my own life, so I decided to pack it myself.

The technique is straightforward: You spread the parachute open, weighing it down with rocks so that the wind doesn't move it around. The next step is carefully folding it up, being sure to remove the rocks as you go.

I was very confident that I had done a great job until shortly into my second jump. When my parachute opened, I was bombarded by heaps of rocks pummelling my head, shoulders, and arms.

Being nearsighted and maybe not too careful, I had unknowingly missed some (a lot!) of the rocks as I folded my parachute, packing them in instead of tossing them out.

Luckily, it's customary to wear a motorcycle helmet when you jump, to protect your head from a tough landing. I discovered it came in handy even when I was way up in the sky. As far as I could tell no one was below me. I looked, but at that point there wouldn't have been anything I could have done to warn someone about the barrage of stones.

The rocks weren't too big, so taking a few hits didn't in any way sour parachuting for me. I had a way better experience than a waitress from a nearby restaurant who made her first jump around the same time I was getting started.

After her parachute opened, the newbie panicked, and although someone on the ground yelled instructions to her through a bullhorn, she steered directly onto a power line at full speed, staring straight ahead the whole time. Her mouth was wide open, as if she was screaming, though no one could hear. I watched her go out of sight behind a little hill. She hit the power line, bounced off and landed on a highway.

A great truck driver somehow saw what was happening. He swerved, stopping his truck to block traffic, and saved her from being run over. An ambulance took her to a nearby hospital. She had no medical insurance, and we took up a collection for her.

Watching the accident was sobering, but not enough to dampen my enthusiasm. On my next jump, I had far fewer rocks, they were smaller, and I was much more relaxed about the whole thing.

After landing closer to the target than my classmates, and being good at drinking beer with more-experienced skydivers afterward, I became the captain of my university's parachuting team.

I loved the thrill and challenge of parachuting and was very enthusiastic about continuing. My eye doctor was excited too, but for a different reason. He pointed out that it was not a good idea for anyone who has had a detached retina to parachute, because a big blow to the head—which could happen—might lead to further detachment and blindness. Disappointing news for me, since I had had a detached retina in each eye when I was younger. I reluctantly gave up my captaincy and the sport. I enjoyed catching up with my parachuting friends for several years and continue to recommend the sport to everyone who hasn't had detached retinas.

During my brief tenure as a skydiver, I got some great advice that I found useful for parachuting and in many vastly different situations since then.

Before my third and final jump, I was still a little nervous about whether my parachute would open, and if I would need to open the backup 'chute as I had been tempted to do the first time.

It would have been a big mess and very dangerous if I had followed my impulse to pop the backup unit. The two canopies could have become entangled, which practically guarantees neither one does its job.

As I worried aloud, a more experienced jumper told me, "Plan for the worst, then be pleasantly surprised if anything else happens."

Later on, I discovered that his tip works on the ground as well as in the air. When I entered the business world, his words of wisdom often came in handy in planning and project management.

To this day I prepare as thoroughly as I can, but I just count on things not working. From that point, I don't worry about it and am pleasantly surprised when things go as they should. I find it much more relaxing to think that way.

* * * * * * * * *

 For a while I tried a career as a sheet metal worker. I took the test, became an apprentice, and was assigned to a good New York City sheet metal firm. Half the time I worked in the company's South Bronx shop, fabricating ducts for heating, ventilation and air conditioning. The rest of the time I was at construction sites installing the ducts we made. I worked on two projects: One was a Midtown Manhattan skyscraper; the other was the North Tower of the World Trade Center.

It was winter, and one of the three WTC floors between the Windows on the World restaurant and the giant rooftop antennae was undergoing a gut renovation. A duct was open to the outside, and all of the other trade guys complained about the freezing wind ripping through the job site. Their griping stopped when the sheet metal worker in charge told them that one of our guys was in the duct—the vortex of the freezing wind—fixing something outside.

That was me.

I was 110 stories up, stretched out horizontally in the narrow passage. From the waist up I was outside, repairing exterior sheet metal. A coworker held onto my legs, ensuring I wouldn't fall out. Besides fixing whatever I was supposed to fix, I also took the time to enjoy the great view. I had a good look around, including straight down to the street, more than 1,000 feet below.

Part of being an apprentice included learning more about working with sheet metal at the union's training site. Everything seemed to be going just fine, until one of the instructors said I needed a letter from my eye doctor saying I could see well enough to be a construction worker. My eye doctor didn't think so, and he refused to write the letter.

I was happy being a tin banger, in fact I still have my tools. I think I was doing a good job. I got along well with my coworkers and bosses.

But maybe the eye doctor was right—maybe I avoided some injuries and prolonged my life by having to choose another line of work.

Years later, I lived and worked near the World Trade Center when it was attacked and destroyed by terrorists in 2001. It was terrifying to be close to the collapsing buildings and escaping through the giant cloud of dust. It was tragic that so many people died. On a much less significant note, I also felt bad that a bit of my handiwork was gone forever.

Laughing to a Longer Life

Laughter is the best medicine. I've found that if you can laugh at your own adventures, you will be healthier, happier, and probably live longer.

There is a sight gag related to puddles in some of the old classic black-and-white Laurel and Hardy movies. One of them walks through a puddle just fine, barely getting his feet wet. The other half of the comedy duo follows, stepping into the same puddle, which is suddenly so deep that he disappears below the surface. I think this routine is hysterical.

Maybe I think it is so funny because I cannot see well enough to judge the depth of a puddle and occasionally go in pretty deep. Never above my head, so far. But once in a while I step in almost up to my knee. Whenever that happens, I think of Laurel and Hardy and laugh. It is not good for your shoes, socks and pants, but it might toughen up your immune system: another plus for health and a longer life span.

* * * * * * * * *

I never admitted it when I was a kid, but when watching cartoons I liked relating to Mr. Magoo's poor eyesight. I enjoyed his misadventures, admired his perseverance, and thought he was funny. I laughed *with* him, rather than *at* him. It is not politically correct, but some funny things happen to those of us with poor vision, so we might as well enjoy an occasional laugh at ourselves.

On the other hand, I am uncomfortable when people with good vision laugh at Mr. Magoo. It always feels like they are laughing at him, and by inference, at me and everyone else with poor eyesight.

* * * * * * * * *

When I was a boy, I thought it would be fun to plant a garden. For my starting project, I wanted to grow something big and tasty. I set my heart on watermelons. We didn't live on a farm or in a rural area, but we had a little side yard, and my ma said it would be OK.

I enthusiastically dug out all the grass in a big square shape, turned the soil, watered everything, and followed the directions on the watermelon seed pack. I was off to a great start.

The bedroom I shared with my brother looked out over the yard, and I often glanced out the window to check on my garden's progress.

Then things got complicated.

Green shoots started coming up all over the place in my little garden patch. I wanted to get rid of the weeds, and at the same time encourage and nourish the watermelons. Which were which? I couldn't tell. Not wanting to accidently pull out any  watermelon plants, I ended up letting everything grow. This turned out to be a bad strategy. Pretty soon the whole space I'd cleared was full of green stuff that did not appear to be baby watermelons. I gave up.

A while later, just as we were waking up one morning, my brother got very excited and pointed out the window: There was a watermelon in the garden! I got very excited. As we both gazed at it through the window, I experienced all the joys of being a successful gardener. He congratulated me, and I ran out to get a closer look.

I picked up the watermelon and was surprised that it had no vines or roots. Then I heard my brother's laughter: He had bought a watermelon and put it in the middle of my patch of weeds.

The watermelon tasted twice as good because of the hearty laugh we shared. I gave up on gardening, but ever since I have enjoyed telling my one gardening story.

Data-Driven Longer Life

In high school I couldn't see well enough to spot friends in the lunchroom cafeteria, and I didn't want to eat alone. My solution was to skip lunch every day and hang out in the school library reading the newspapers. This turned me into much more of a loner in high school than I wanted to be, but I developed a lifelong interest in news and news analysis.

Like many others with bad eyes, I am interested in news about potential medical break-throughs that could lead to better vision. That interest naturally expands into a broader interest in news on general health, diet, and exercise. All of which has the benefit of creating or reinforcing good habits for a healthier and longer life.

Getting Lost for a Longer Life

A lot of us poor-vision people are great walkers, because of factors such as not having a driver's license, or making a habit of taking the stairs because we cannot find the elevator or read some elevator buttons.

We're also great at getting lost. We might excel at reading maps, but that only works if you don't have difficulty seeing them. Not being able to read some street signs or recognize some landmarks also contributes to a tendency to get lost. We might take longer routes over steeper, more rugged terrain because we don't see a more direct or smoother path.

All this extra walking could also mean extra carrying. If we are carrying things while walking farther, it is even better exercise, again leading to a longer, healthier life.

Spending a lot of time walking and running also yields the side benefits of better balance and occasional unexpected minor adventures.

It can be exciting not being able to tell the difference on a sidewalk or road between dark spots, dark litter, leaves, shadows, holes, bumps, dirt, ice, and puddles. This is especially true at night. The good news is that you develop quick balance adjustment with each foot landing.

My high school's cross-country team went out of town for a week of preseason training in the Vermont mountains. On one afternoon run, we were told to keep running straight until taking the first right.

It was a long run in a remote country area, and after a while everyone was spread out, some ahead of me, some behind me. All of them out of sight.

I was enjoying the run and the scenery, though I had to slow down a bit to work my way through a happy party of newlyweds and guests spilling out of a church, onto the lawn and road. Once I left the crowd behind, I picked up the pace a bit and continued on my merry way.

I enjoyed lots more pretty countryside, plenty of hills, but no right-hand turns. No teammates passed me. I didn't pass any teammates. I was getting tired but had no idea how far I had run. It was starting to get dark, so I turned around and started jogging back, slowing to a walk as I got even more worn out.

Meanwhile, my teammates and coach were getting a bit worried as they waited for me at the meetup point. They drove around looking for me, and called the local hospital, morgue, and police. I was surprised when a police car stopped and asked if I was Ken Brandt. I was also very happy that the policeman gave me a ride back to the team.

I had completely missed the right-hand turn that was behind the happy crowd celebrating with the newlyweds.

Extra scenery, more running, good view of a fun wedding party, a bit of a challenge, and a friendly rescue: generally, all good!

Optometrists always live long lives…
It's because they dilate.

Eye puns aren't really puns.
They're optical allusions.

I'm not saying my eyesight is getting worse
but yesterday, in the car, I spent 20 minutes
letting a hedgehog cross the road.
I carried on driving when I discovered that
it was a pinecone.

Chapter 2

Science to the Rescue

> *"I've learned that fear limits you and your vision. It serves as blinders to what may be just a few steps down the road for you. The journey is valuable, but believing in your talents, your abilities, and your self-worth can empower you to walk down an even brighter path. Transforming fear into freedom – how great is that?"*
>
> *–Soledad O'Brien*

I love modern research, science, and medicine. If it wasn't for modern research, science, and medicine, I would be completely blind.

Serious researchers are trying to figure out ways to repair and replace missing and damaged eyeball parts. I strongly support continued eyeball research. I can tell you from experience: this stuff is great.

I have always had poor vision in my good eye, and significantly worse vision in my bad eye. I've had six eye operations, including a detached retina operation in each eye, and a cataract operation in each eye. I was legally blind for parts of my life.

Welcome to my vision roller-coaster ride. My eyesight has had a lot of up and downs, even more so prior to the timeframe of this chart.

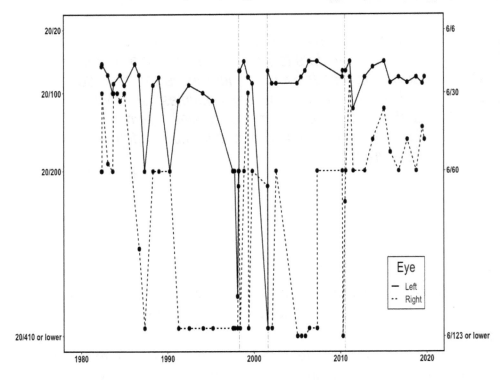

KEN'S CORRECTED EYESIGHT
For a detailed explanation, see Appendix: Understanding the Eye Chart

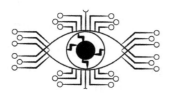 I was born three-months prema-
ture, weighing 3 pounds, 7 ounces
(1.56 kg.) at birth, and soon dropped
to 2 pounds, 14 ounces (1.30 kg.).
At that time—1954—many coun-
tries, including the U.S., were using oxygen tents to help keep
premature babies alive. I spent my early days in one at Magee
Hospital in Pittsburgh, Pennsylvania, now known as UPMC
Magee-Womens Hospital.

A 1951 Australian study showed that too high a percent-
age of oxygen in the tent led to blindness. It took a while to
conduct confirming studies, discredit other theories, and for the
word to spread. In the meantime, however, the oxygen blinded
many babies.

It wasn't easy for researchers to find a balance between
enough oxygen to keep kids alive, but not so much as to cause
blindness. Magee was one of the first three hospitals in the
U.S. to learn from the studies and lower the oxygen level
for preemies.

I was one of the first babies born in the U.S. where the doctors
were successfully able to give me enough oxygen to survive,
but not so much that I would go blind. Growing up, I had worse
vision than any non-blind person that my friends, schoolteachers, sports coaches, university professors, bosses, or coworkers
knew. Nevertheless, my situation is much luckier than being
dead or blind.

As with quite a few premature babies, my eyes did not have
time to develop as many rods and cones as an infant born at
full term would have, so I have always been nearsighted. I have
also always had lazy (sort of crossed) eyes. When I'm tired, they

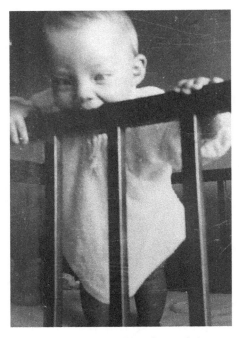

Pre-glasses: An energetic, active, and strong baby, who broke two cribs.

are especially lazy / crossed.

When I was a year old, I wore an eye patch to strengthen my eyes, alternating between the left and right. At 2, I graduated from the patches and got my first pair of glasses.

At 4, my eyes got much worse, and patching was briefly reinstated. I got stronger prescription glasses and had an exploratory operation to see why my eyes had gotten worse. My eyes got better, then worse, then went back to where they were. The doctors couldn't explain it.

At 10 my eyes got a bit better, again no medical explanation.

I had two of the very first successful detached retina operations, first one eye, then the other. The first, when I was 11, was an old-style procedure, in which I was strapped facing-downward to a bed that was suspended from the ceiling of the operating room. The process changed by the time my other eye was operated on two years later.

The repair operations saved my vision, but my vision got worse.

At one point I briefly tried hard contact lenses. They worked great at first, but after a short while began to bother my eyes, so I went back to glasses.

With glasses: early on and in third grade

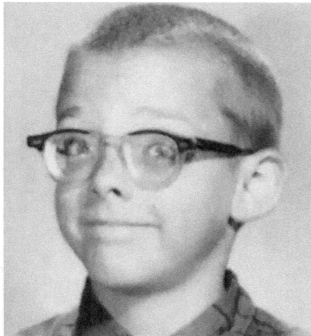

**With glasses:
in high school**

At 26 I wore glasses and sported a blond mustache. A local store was selling a really cheap plastic Groucho Marx disguise, consisting of a goofy one-piece combination of glasses frames, nose, and black mustache. My Christmas stocking-stuffer plan was to buy a bunch of them, paint the mustaches yellow to

match my blond one, and call them Ken Brandt disguise kits. A bunch of goofy clones of me could have been running around for a while. However, my plan fell through because six months prior to that holiday season I successfully switched from glasses to soft contact lenses.

Groucho Marx: Comic and movie star

That was very exciting: no glasses to fog over, and a big vision improvement in rain, snow, and splattered mud.

To correct a slow clouding over of my left eye, I had a successful cataract operation at age 44. Cataract operations replace the eye's natural lens (the part of the eye that clouds over) with an embedded plastic lens. If you are nearsighted, like me, the closer the lens is to your eye the more it helps—and the lens cannot get any closer than embedded. After a cataract operation you no longer need a contact lens, which makes life easier. However, because the embedded plastic lens doesn't adjust to different distances the way a natural lens does, I started using reading glasses.

Three years later a cloudy membrane developed behind my embedded cataract lens and was removed with yttrium-aluminum-garnet (YAG) laser posterior capsulotomy surgery. You get eye-drop anesthesia, but it still hurts a bit. Nevertheless, it is very cool surgery. You are awake, sitting up, and seeing though

21

the eye as the doctor uses a laser to create a hole in your eye's cloudy membrane to improve your vision. Since you want the laser to drill in the right place, you try very hard to look in the right direction, keep your eye steady, and keep from looking away. You hear a crackling sound and it looks like you are rocketing at hyper-warp speed through a colorful space-time wormhole in a science-fiction adventure movie.

At 55, I had a successful cataract operation in my right eye.

I have been very lucky that advances in science and medicine have come along just in time. Figuring out the right amount of oxygen for premature babies and how to perform detached retina operations saved my sight. Glasses and contact lenses have been a tremendous help to me. I had highly successful, but by then gloriously routine, cataract operations.

Between cataract operations: honeymooning with the wonderful Judy Roberts Brandt

What did the eye say after it got glasses?
Eye'm back!

Ever been to an optimistic optometrist?
They'll tell you that your glasses are half full.

Patient: Doctor, will I be able to read after wearing glasses?
Eye Doctor: Yes, of course, why not!
Patient (joyfully): Oh! How nice it will be,
I have been illiterate for so long!

Where do you take someone who has been injured
in a Peek-a-Boo accident?
The ICU!

Chapter 3

Adventure and Discovery

> *"One day, your life will flash before your eyes. Make sure it is worth watching."*
>
> *–Gerard Way*

Poor vision makes most things more of an adventure. When I started writing this book, some friends asked why I like parachuting, scuba diving, horseback riding, spelunking, and other semi-adventurous activities, despite my bad eyes.

I have always enjoyed things that require bits of daring and courage, but never thought about why.

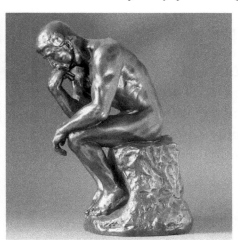

After thinking about it for a few days, I came up with three possible reasons: genetics, encouragement, and poor eyesight itself.

First, there might be some courage, grit, and sense of adventure in my genes. One of my great-great-grandfathers was captain of a whaling

Why?

25

ship; a great-grandfather captained a clipper ship. One of my great-grandmothers emigrated from Ireland at age 13, traveling in steerage class to Canada, then moving to Boston, all on her own. One of my grandfathers was an infantryman in trench warfare in WWI. My father served as a Marine during the Korean War. Both earned medals for bravery.

Second, I was very lucky to have been encouraged to do whatever positive activities interested me in my early years. I was brought up to believe that pretty much anything is possible if you work hard. My parents never had a single discussion with me while I was growing up regarding limits on what I might or might not be able to do as an adult with poor vision. Plus, unbeknownst to me, my ma prevented any schoolteachers, relatives or others from having such discussions with me.

As a result, I never even thought about limitations until I got to the age where everyone else could get a driver's license. However, my ma did discourage me from doing things that might further damage my vision—like parachuting—which was very reasonable.

Lastly, poor eyesight itself can make you more courageous. "Bold" can mean facing danger or adventure when you don't know what the danger or adventure will be. If you are not sure what you are looking at, you get a lot of practice being bold. If you are used to being bold, it is only a tiny step further to being brave – which can mean facing danger or adventure even when you know what you are getting into.

That's my three-part theory.

Dive Bomb Practice

I was a summer camp counselor when I was in high school, and one year I led a hike to the little local airport and went on a brief plane ride. I sat next to the pilot in the copilot seat, the only other seat in the plane.

In just a few minutes we flew over the camp, and the pilot asked if I wanted to steer for a bit. I did, and immediately started dive bomb swoops over the camp. He didn't let me dive as low as I wanted to go, but it was fun, and then he flew us back to the airport.

After hiking back to camp, we found out that everyone was excited about the dive bombing and that the camp had called the airport, local police, state police, and the Federal Aviation Administration to report the pilot. I still feel bad about that. As far as I know, the camp never let another counselor do that flight again. Being nearsighted, perhaps I was dive bombing a little lower than I thought.

Spelunking (Caving)

When I was in my 20s and 30s, I enjoyed spelunking with friends in West Virginia and upper New York State. These were not tourist caves with marked routes and guides, but some were unofficially marked or graffitied with lots of contradictory directions. Each cave was off the beaten path, and none had safety features, tourist guides, park rangers, officials, or lighting of any type.

Inside the caves were tunnels, cliffs, caverns, ponds, streams, waterfalls, and lots of ups, downs, twists, and turns, all over rocks and mud. It was awesome. All of it was challenging and parts were beautiful.

Once you go into one of these caves it is unbelievably dark. Imagine a cloudy night with no moon and no outside light; you go home, close all the curtains, turn off all the lights, get into bed, and tuck your head completely underneath a bunch of blankets. Then you close your eyes. That is still way brighter than being deep inside a cave. Your eyes and mind may trick you a bit with an old image because your brain refuses to believe you cannot see anything while your eyes are open. But trust me, you can't.

Once while spelunking in a cave near Albany, New York, with two of my best friends, John and Paul, we got completely lost. We had no idea which way to go to get back to the entrance— up, down, this way, that way. We decided each of us would test different paths.

My route was up a very narrow tunnel, a space too small to crawl in. I had to move forward on my stomach, pulling myself forward with one arm ahead of me and one at my side, pushing myself a bit with my ankle muscles. I went pretty far, didn't see anything, then backed out, which took a while.

John wanted to double-check, so he did the same thing. He came back to report that I had gotten to within just inches of the end of the tunnel but must not have seen the end. He could tell by the marks I left in the dirt. I should have stuck it out and gone a bit further. That was a good life lesson.

We always wore caving helmets: a hard hat with a carbide lamp attached to the front. The lamps are made of two chambers: There's water in the upper chamber, which drips down to the calcium carbide in the chamber below, which reacts to form

Celebrating a cave adventure with good friends John (left) and Paul (center)

acetylene gas. The acetylene gas shoots out through the middle of a reflector, which is lit, and the flame provides the light. It is exciting and fun to walk, crawl, and climb around in the dark with a flame on your head.

While in that same Albany cave, the water in my caving helmet ran low. John, Paul, and I formed a small circle, so their helmet lamps enabled me to see as I added water to my helmet lamp. I was holding my helmet in one hand while pouring the water from a canteen into my helmet's water chamber with the other.

Paul has good vision, but it was dark, and he had not seen this done before, so he leaned in to get a closer look as I was pouring, and accidently set my hair on fire. John and Paul thought it was pretty dramatic being very close to an unexpected fire against a pitch-black background. The first I knew of it was my two good friends instantly coming to my rescue by pounding my head to put out the flames, yelling, "Fire!"

I used both arms to protect my head from their pounding and poured water from the already-open canteen onto my head. We each reacted so quickly that to our amazement, my hair was only singed. I thanked them for saving me, Paul apologized for accidentally setting me on fire, and we all had a good laugh. I finished filling up my helmet lamp, and we went further into the cave. The next day, the singe wasn't even noticeable (at least to me).

Another time I was in a West Virginia cave with John and other friends when my helmet light went out. I was in front, with my friends following behind. Instead of stopping, even though it was pitch black and I couldn't see where I was going, I took one more step, which turned out to be off a little cliff. It was about 10 feet (three-plus meters) down onto some rocks. A bit to my surprise, I was completely unhurt.

I yelled out: "Stop walking!" John, who was right behind me, wondered how I had disappeared. But he didn't take another step, which was nice, as he would have landed on me.

Giddyup!

Horseback riding can be a lot of fun. For me, that's partly because of a bit of teamwork that many riders may take for granted: The horse probably has good vision and looks where it's going, so I don't have to see everything.

My Montana ranching cousins say that you need to

accidently fall off your horse three times before you can be a cowboy. I must be a real cowboy, as I managed to do it four times.

The first instance was when I was a little kid. My cousin Steve was leading an unsaddled horse out of the stable at his suburban New York farm, and asked if I wanted to try riding it. The horse's back was way above my head, and I climbed up onto something so I could mount it bareback. With no saddle and Steve holding the reins, I had nothing to hang onto.

I had never done this before, but I had seen plenty of Western movies, so I had no worries. After about 15 feet, I fell off onto a stone walkway. I laughed so much, they gave me another go: This time I had a saddle and held the reins, and I did much better.

After that I had no trouble staying on a horse. Unless you count a few experiences at my cousins' ranch in Montana.

When herding cattle, the animals get hungry. Then, one by one, they decide it would be a good idea to go back to have some grass at the last place they ate, so they turn around and run in the opposite direction. Cowboys and cowgirls have to gallop very close to the rogue cow, get a tiny bit ahead and make a really sharp turn, forcing it back toward the herd.

It's fun and exciting, and it works just fine. Unless you haven't cinched your saddle tight enough, in which case you go flying off your horse while making that really sharp galloping turn. I was guilty of this twice at the ranch, once when I was 18 and again about a decade later.

Another time, four of us were partway back from a cattle drive when my cousin Maynard, the head of the ranch, and another guy decided to go for a beer. They handed over their horses to my cousin Meg (Maynard's daughter) and me to take home. Meg and I each had one hand busy with our own horse's reins and the other hand occupied with the reins of the horse we were leading.

She had a chore to do before going back, so she headed off, leaving me on my own.

Galloping is much more fun than walking—remember, I like to go fast—so I picked up the pace. It was my first time galloping while leading another horse, and as we broke into a run, the horse in the rear didn't get off to as quick a start. I found myself leaning back, with my left arm fully stretched out behind me, hanging on to the reins of the horse I was leading.

Even in that awkward position, practically flying down the road felt great, until my saddle started slipping. But I had to keep galloping at full speed. I had given my own horse so much slack that I couldn't rein him in. I couldn't use my other hand to gather the reins, since I was still reaching back, holding onto the other horse.

To regain control of the horse I was riding, I had to eliminate some of the slack in the reins. So, I started tossing them in the air just a bit and catching them a little closer, aiming to eventually get the lines taut enough to slow down. I had been told to never, ever let go of the reins, but I figured this was OK. I was slowly making my way to the point where I would be able to rein in my horse. But I didn't make it. My saddle suddenly slipped completely.

Still clutching both sets of reins, I kicked my feet out of the stirrups and was dragged between the two galloping horses, down a rocky dirt road. That stopped pretty soon, as dragging me by the reins must have been unpleasant for them.

Meg very nicely galloped over to see if I was OK, which amazingly enough, I was.

Not all of my Montana-related adventures involved four or eight legs. Before going west, I needed to learn to drive, which was very exciting for someone who does not see well enough to get a driver's license. My brother helped me give it a try in the driveway at home, and my friend John drove me to a big practice area: the parking lot of Shea Stadium, where the New York Mets played baseball from 1964 till 2008. My attempts in the driveway did not go too well, especially parking. We had to

quit practicing at the mighty Shea once the police came.

At the ranch I drove only in fields and on small roads (with one little exception on a state highway). I did

Driving a tractor

get to operate some great stuff: tractors pulling different things, pickups, and big trucks with 16 gears (I used every one of them).

I only got into two accidents. Once I drove a pickup truck into a big irrigation ditch. My cousin Maynard had to tow it out. Another time I backed that same pick-up (with the tailgate open) into something, just missing Maynard's son, my cousin Randy. The tailgate was crunched at bit. Luckily, Randy was aware of my driving ability, and smart enough to not stand directly in front of or behind anything I was driving.

High-Wire Act

Sometimes poor eyesight helps you earn admiration and respect accidently or unknowingly. When my friend Deb was playing in her neighborhood as a kid, she and her friends went to a nearby home construction site. No one was working there, and there was no fence, but there was a large, deep hole that had been dug for the basement. Across the big pit was a single long plank, not connected to anything. There was no walkway, no handrail, just a wobbly, skinny wooden board. All the other kids were too scared to cross it. Thanks to a combination of Deb's adventurous spirit and lack of depth perception (she couldn't see the difference between the height of the plank and the bottom of the hole), she boldly skipped right across the length of the board, becoming a legend within her peer group.

Finding Friends and Meeting New People

Like many others, I dislike being alone in a crowd. Unlike others, I cannot recognize people from a distance. If it is a meeting with name tags, I cannot read the name tags. I will be alone until I find someone I know, which may take me a little while.

My willingness to brave a crowd works in two good ways. First, more so than people who can see well, the situation forces me to have the courage to introduce myself to strangers. This works out well because it is almost always more relaxing, fun, and interesting to be talking to someone than to be looking for someone.

Second, just by being in the crowd, the people I do know can spot me and come over to say hello. If I had stayed away, they would not have noticed me. Everyone—especially people with poor vision—really likes it when friends spot us somewhere and go out of their way to come up to say hi.

Stepping Up and Stepping Down

Stairways can be tough to judge. Going up is tougher for farsighted people, because the stairs are closer to their eyes. Going down is tougher for nearsighted people because the stairs are farther from their eyes.

It can be hard to see where one step starts and another stops, particularly if there is more than one color or design on each step, and especially if the design on each step involves stripes parallel to the steps.

Luckily there is a counterintuitive, but easy solution: Don't look at the stairs. Just stay within reach of the handrail, estimate each step's distance or depth, and go for it. It is amazing how comfortable and easy it is. Of course, you do have to pay some attention, so that you know when you reach a landing, corner, or big body of water.

Too Close, But Comfortable

When I lived in Baltimore, Maryland, a cataract was slowly clouding over my left eye, which sees much better than my right eye. It took me a while to figure out what was happening. For a month or so I thought that my right eye was getting much better because it could see better than my left eye. I was happy with my analysis and what I thought was a positive development, so I didn't check with an eye doctor.

Around that time, as I was walking home from work my route took me past Baltimore's beautiful Inner Harbor. I was wearing a business suit. The Inner Harbor is deep enough for

fairly large ships to dock. It was a very still night—no wind, no waves, so the water was totally calm, dead flat.

Surrounding that part of the harbor are some different levels of walking spaces that gradually step down to the water.

Foot in the air, I was in the process of taking one more step down to the next level, when I realized it was water rather than walkway. The harbor was as flat and unmoving as the paths around it, and that just about faked me out. I barely managed to pull back and avoid walking into the water. I would have been cold and a mess. No one was around, but I was still a little embarrassed. Luckily, I get over these things quickly.

In the past my eye doctor had advised me to wait as long as possible before having a cataract operation. I had lived in New York before Baltimore. When I moved back to the city—to Brooklyn, this time—from Maryland, I noticed a big change in my vision. I realized I had to get much closer to read the street signs than the last time I lived there.

On my third day back in town, I had to work late. It was my first time going home to my new apartment after dark. It was a beautiful neighborhood, but all the buildings looked pretty much the same at night. Much to my surprise, I couldn't read the street signs or many of the house numbers.

Since I was still new to the area, finding my way home turned into a fun challenge. I knew my address and the names of the streets near my apartment, but this was before phones had map apps to rely on. I was in no rush, I had plenty of time to wander around. It felt like an interesting way to explore my new Brooklyn stomping ground, though I hoped I had not wandered out of it.

I walked past some repair guys working on utility lines under the sidewalk. They were very friendly, especially the one who suggested I watch out, as I was just one step away from an open manhole. I was happy with that advice.

I was relieved to eventually find my apartment (no, I did not ask anyone for directions). When I got there I discovered that my front door key didn't work, but that is a different story, unrelated to poor vision.

The next day, I scheduled a cataract operation. I spent that whole evening walking around the same area, but this time I knew where I was in relation to my apartment, and I memorized everything.

The Brooklyn Bridge

What do you call low-vision dinosaurs?
Douthinktheysaurus

What happened to the lab technician when he
fell into the lens grinder?
He made a spectacle of himself.

A guy was in an optometrist shop the other day...
guess who he bumped into? Everyone!

Where is the eye located? Between the H and the J.

What do you call a fish with no eyes?
A fsh.

What do you call a deer with no eyes?
No eye-deer.

Chapter 4

Successful People with Poor Eyesight

I do my best – some days are way better than others – to live by my three favorite quotes. This is the first of them:

"It is not the critic who counts, not the man who points out how the strong man stumbled, or where the doer of deeds could have done better. The credit belongs to the man who is actually in the arena: whose face is marred by dust and sweat and blood; who strives valiantly; who errs, and comes short again and again; who knows the great enthusiasms, the great devotions; who spends himself in a worthy cause; who, at the best, knows in the end the triumph of high achievement, and who, at the worst, if he fails, at least fails while daring greatly."

–Theodore Roosevelt

Throughout history and into the present, hundreds of millions of successful people have had poor eyesight. They did not let their eyesight stop them, and you shouldn't either. Here is a small but inspiring sample of people who wore glasses.

Ben Franklin (1709-1790)

A Founding Father of the U.S., as well as a diplomat, author, and inventor. His inventions include the lightning rod, swim fins, an improved urinary catheter, the glass armonica, the Franklin stove, and bifocal glasses.

Catherine the Great (1729-1796)

Her reign was considered Russia's golden age, during which the country was revitalized, grew larger and stronger, and gained recognition as one of the great powers of Europe.

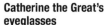

Catherine the Great's eyeglasses

Susan B. Anthony (1820-1906)

A leading U.S. suffragette and activist for gender and racial equality. The 19th Constitutional Amendment, often called the Susan B. Anthony amendment, gave American women the right to vote.

Teddy Roosevelt (1858-1919)

An American president, historian, explorer, Nobel Peace Prize winner, and leader of the Rough Riders. He greatly expanded the national parks and forests in the U.S., was a driving force in building the Panama Canal, and inspired the creation of the ever-popular teddy bear.

Mahatma Gandhi (1869-1948)

This Indian activist used nonviolent civil disobedience to lead India from British colonial rule to independence. He inspired nonviolent movements for civil rights and freedom across the world.

Katharine Burr Blodgett (1898-1979)

An American physicist, whose research yielded significant improvements for eyeglasses, camera lenses, and more. She invented "invisible" or nonreflective glass, coatings for glass, and a method for using a color gauge to measure molecular glass coatings to one millionth of an inch.

Dom DiMaggio, "The Little Professor" (1917-2009)

A seven-time All-Star Major League Baseball player, he was a tremendous hitter and fielder. He played center field for the Boston Red Sox for his entire career, from 1940-1953.

Martin Luther King Jr. (1929-1968)

A key leader of the American civil rights movement, an advocate for nonviolent protest, and a Nobel Peace Prize winner. His "I Have a Dream" speech for equality is among the greatest public addresses of all time.

Martin Luther King Jr.'s eyeglasses

Steve Jobs (1955-2011)

An American technology pioneer, visionary, investor, and business leader. He was also the chief executive officer and founder or cofounder of Apple, NeXT, and Pixar.

Stephen Hawking (1942-2018)

This English theoretical physicist theorized cosmology as a union of the general theory of relativity and quantum mechanics. He also wrote the international bestseller *A Brief History of Time*.

My only plan for today is to get new glasses,
then I'll see what happens.

How much do you weigh?
Precisely 165 pounds (75 kg) when I'm wearing
my glasses.
What about when you are not wearing your glasses?
No idea. Can't read the scale

Why did the phone wear glasses?
Because it lost all its contacts!

Optician: You need glasses.
Patient: But I'm wearing glasses.
Optician: Then I need glasses.

Woman: My grandfather lived for 96 years and he
never used glasses.
Man: Yes, I know, some people in my family also
drink directly from the bottle

Chapter 5

Imagination, Creativity, and Focus

> "You can't depend on your eyes when your imagination is out of focus."
>
> —Mark Twain

Foresight and Vision

Twice I worked at firms that had very extensive employee-evaluation processes. My favorite evaluation category—designed to rate your strategy abilities—was called Foresight  and Vision. I always ranked well in this category, which I still find hilarious.

Making It Up

It is easy to recognize your curled-up sleeping dog or cat on the floor and think nothing of it. Until you realize that your pet is outside, and you were looking at your sweatshirt. Makes you wonder how much else you are taking for granted.

Sometimes you imagine correctly, sometimes not. Either way, you must think creatively every time you look around. Plus, you must be open-minded enough to readjust your assessment when you get a better understanding of what you are looking at, and have a good enough sense of humor to laugh at yourself when you get it wrong.

School

My education, from elementary school through college, took place in the days of blackboards, way before many of the great visual technology advancements of today. Getting through school without being able to read most of what the teacher wrote on the board, especially in subjects involving formulas and spelling, was a challenge. The good news was that it built some helpful lifelong skills and approaches: good listening, an active imagination, and putting in extra work outside class. I also got in the habit of sitting up front.

My brother, who has good vision, is two years younger than me, so was a couple of grades behind me in the same schools. Years after each of us finished high school, I learned that when teachers realized we're related, they would assume he had poor vision too, so would make him sit in the front row. It was like he had done something wrong by being my brother. I still feel bad about that.

Focus and Concentration

Better focus and concentration can be among the advantages of poor eyesight. People with good eyesight see a lot more of everything, including many distractions. People with poor vision see fewer distractions, which increases our likelihood of unbroken stretches of focus and concentration, enabling more effective working, reading, and learning.

If a person is nearsighted, this is doubly true. Nearsighted people must be much closer to whatever they are looking at, so whatever we're focusing on—a book, phone, computer screen, sheet music—blocks out our view of practically everything else. More things obscured from view equals fewer distractions, making it even easier to focus and concentrate.

Magic

Some things, such as magic tricks, are more fun for people with low vision. Magicians use sleight of hand and other visually deceptive routines to entertain. The more visually deceptive the magic trick, the more entertaining it is. People with poor vision are easier to visually deceive, so are easier to entertain. We are the perfect audience for amateur magicians

and people just learning magic tricks: To us, the tricks are just as good as those done by professional magicians.

Poker

Unfortunately, those of us with poor vision are more susceptible to card sharks and cheats, so it's best to stick to occasional, low-stakes games with friends.

With that said, one summer I spent a lot of time cheating at poker with a few buddies. We all cheated. We didn't bet, and we only played against one another. The challenge was to see who could hide and add cards to their hand without being spotted, who could spot others hiding and adding cards, and who could shuffle the deck so that the cards came up in the desired order. I was OK at shuffling, but disastrous at hiding and spotting, but we all had a great time.

Trompe L'oeil

Similarly, trompe l'oeil, is cooler and more fun for people with low vision. Trompe l'oeil (the French phrase means "deceives the eye") is an optical illusion painting technique that transforms flat surfaces into realistic three-dimensional scenes. A standard ceiling could appear to be the inside of a dome decorated with spectacular ancient art. A sidewalk could be transformed into a view from the edge of the Grand Canyon.

The worse your eyesight, the more you use your imagination, so the more three dimensional and realistic trompe l'oeil looks.

Tromp L'oeil Example from a Roman Palazzo

Two for the Price of One

For a while I was wearing a contact lens in only my good eye, because wearing one in my bad eye didn't make any noticeable difference. Every morning I got up, got ready to go to work, put in my contact lens, and left the house. One day my eye started to bother me a bit, but I figured it would go away. Instead, it got much worse, and by midmorning my contact

lens was killing me. I knew I needed to take it out, so I decided to go home to get a spare.

As I left the office and walked toward the elevator, my eye bothered me so much that I took the contact out and put it in my pocket. I knew this would wreck the soft lens (I didn't care) and that I would need to get home via subway without being able to see well (which I was a bit concerned about). Then, for a brief while, I thought a miracle had occurred. Before I got all the way to the elevator, my eye felt much better and I could see fine. I was very excited.

Then I realized that I had accidently slept with my contact lens in, and put another one on top of it in the morning. On the way to the elevator I had unintentionally—and luckily!— somehow managed to remove only one of the two lenses. Even though my eyesight didn't miraculously improve, it was fun believing it for a short while.

Eye Patches

Eye patches were a necessary pain for strengthening of the opposite eye when I was very young, and again years later after some of my eye operations. Sometimes a white gauze bandage for maximum eye protection at first, leading to the much more cool black adventurer-pirate eye patch. A few times I had an eye patch over one eye while wearing glasses so that I could see better with the other eye. It looked ridiculous but was still sort of fun. Anytime I think about eye patches, I cannot help but think about pirates and pirate aye jokes.

A pirate walks into a bar and the bartender says, "Hey, I haven't seen you in a while. What happened, you look terrible!"

"What do you mean?" the pirate replies, "I'm fine."

The bartender says, "But what about that wooden leg? You didn't have that before."

"Well," says the pirate, "We were in a battle at sea and a cannonball hit my leg, but the surgeon fixed me up, and I'm fine, really."

"Yeah," says the bartender, "But what about that hook? Last time I saw you, you had both hands."

"Well," says the pirate, "We were in another battle and we boarded the enemy ship. I was in a sword fight and my hand was cut off, but the surgeon fixed me up with this hook, and I feel great, really."

"Oh," says the bartender, "What about that eye patch? Last time you were in here you had both eyes."

"Well," says the pirate, "One day when we were at sea, some birds were flying over the ship. I looked up, and one of them pooped in my eye."

"So?" replied the bartender, "What happened? You couldn't have lost an eye just from some bird poop!"

"Well," says the pirate sadly, "I wasn't really used to the hook yet..."

Why do pirates say, "Aye, aye, Captain"?
Two ayes are better than one.

How do pirates prefer to communicate?
Aye to aye!

What did the pirate say when he turned 80?
Aye matey.

Chapter 6

Public Speaking and Sports

> *"If there are any of you at the back who do not hear me, please don't raise your hands because I am also nearsighted."*
>
> *–W. H. Auden*

Public Speaking

Public speaking, which is terrifying for many people, can be easier for people with bad vision. For us, big audiences aren't any more intimidating than small ones. I can see only a few people in the crowd anyway, so adding a bunch that I cannot see doesn't matter.

Some speakers find it annoying if the lighting prevents them from seeing the audiences' faces. However, those of us with bad vision are already comfortable judging people's reaction solely by whether the laughter and applause are in the right places.

Poor vision can be a motivator to prepare more thoroughly and design a more interesting presentation. I have difficulty seeing my own notes, so I memorize the outline and content of my speech, which results in a better presentation. Since it is hard for me to read my own slides, I am less likely to fall into the boring-speaker trap of standing there reading slides to people who can read them for themselves. Instead my speeches follow the general outline of the slides, emphasizing the key points and including additional anecdotes, making the presentations much more interesting and professional.

I developed these habits because of my vision, but any speaker can adopt them for better presentations.

Sometimes when giving speeches I accidently skip a few of my PowerPoint slides or discuss them in a different order than shown on the screen. This can still work out fine, for several reasons. Since I am unaware of any mix up, I remain relaxed. The disparity keeps the audience on its toes, guessing and thinking a bit more. When—and if!—I realize what's going on with the slides, I explain what happened and laugh; the audience always gives me the benefit of the doubt and laughs along with me, and that forges a stronger connection.

After a speech there is often a question-and-answer period. I always like Q&A, but I like it even more if someone else picks the people in the audience to ask questions. First, I probably don't see some people who are signaling that they have a question. Second, my slightly crossed eyes confuse everyone, so they don't always know which person I am looking at or pointing to for the next question. Third, having someone else choose who to call on allows me to focus on the topic and give better-thought-out answers to questions. I am not partly distracted by watching for whose hand has been in the air the longest.

No Need to See It

The flip side of giving a speech is listening to a speech. Happily, for people with poor eyesight, there is usually no need to see the PowerPoints. Most speakers literally read or come very close to reading their slides verbatim. Those of us with poor vision get to skip this boring duplication.

Batting

As a kid, I sometimes played in neighborhood or family soft-ball games, usually with way more than nine or ten players per side. As an outfielder I could hear the crack of the bat hitting the ball, but I usually couldn't see where the ball was going until way too late. In those situations, sometimes I was one of five or six other outfielders, and someone else would go for it.

As an infielder, I liked to play third base or shortstop, which I found very exciting. I was much closer to the batter, and a hit ball seemed to reach me very, very quickly. I was OK, but not great.

I liked playing catcher the best: For me, the pitched ball is much easier to follow. I was always a bit worried about getting accidently hit in the back of the head with the bat (not a good thing if you have had a detached retina), but luckily that never happened.

As a young batter I was very good. I batted lefty and didn't swing until I was positive the ball was in the strike zone, which

I wasn't sure of until it had almost reached me. Consequently, I always swung late, so my hits were always line drives just over the third baseman's head. No matter how many times in a row a lefty hits a line drive over the third baseman's head, no one expects it to happen again, which is great. I almost always got a single or double.

Then, things changed: I switched from glasses to contact lenses, and I could see everything a bit better. After that I would see the ball sooner, swing sooner, and usually hit the ball directly to the center fielder, who would not have to take a single step. So ended my one- or two-game-a-year softball glory days.

Hand-Eye Coordination

One of my favorite theories is that people with bad vision have great hand-eye coordination. Nearsighted people see objects later, like a ball they are trying to catch or hit, so they must react quicker than people who see it sooner. Farsighted people see the ball's initial arc, but still need to catch or hit it as it gets closer and becomes harder to see.

The same holds true for other athletic moves. The lower the vision, the more a person must rely on faster hand-eye or foot-eye coordination to do the same athletic task. Plus, the more one practices fast hand-eye coordination, the better it gets.

Note: Better hand-eye coordination works for many, but not all types of poor vision. For example, it works well for some nearsighted and farsighted people, but not so well for some with poor depth perception.

Start Your Engines

As someone who doesn't see well enough to have a driver's license, I think it is very interesting that I have never met anyone who considers themselves a below-average driver. A very few think they are average, and all the rest think they are above average.

When I was in high school and college, many of my friends had pretty bad cars. As a result, I set what might be a record: While riding in a bunch of different friends' cars, we broke down in every state bordering the Atlantic from Massachusetts to Virginia, plus Washington, D.C.

Brian Walsh at Daytona International Speedway

On the other hand, my uncle Jerry and my cousin Brian were both SCCA and IMSA race-car drivers, and never broke down when I was along for the ride. The rides were always on a regular road, not a racetrack. As a passenger with either of them they are clearly above-average drivers—much more aware of every car around them and driving more smoothly and safely then others. For a short time my uncle stored his race car in my family's garage, which was super cool.

Sometimes I was lucky enough to watch races from the pits at Lime Rock Park in Lakeville, Connecticut, which was very exciting. I had a pit pass, but of course I didn't do anything. The experts in the pit crew did all the work on the cars, so my "job" was to stay out of the way, cheer, and offer encouragement.

Every once in a while, I'd leave the pits to hit the concession stand and bring back hot dogs for anyone who wanted one. My uncle later told me I was very much appreciated by the drivers and mechanics, and not just for the combination of making hot dogs runs and being friendly. They also liked that I was the only non-racing person who never, ever asked a single "I have a funny sound, rattle, or problem with my car, what do you think it is?" type of question.

Sharing a Bommie

I am a certified scuba diver, and my wife likes to snorkel. Both of us enjoy the fun fact that dive masks make everything underwater look bigger and closer.

There are coral reefs shaped like tall, wide underwater columns—aka bommies—near Australia's Great Barrier Reef. When we are circling a bommie with our diving and snorkeling buddies and groups, she is near the surface, while I am farther below. We share the same view when she is 20 to 35 feet away from whatever beautiful coral and colorful fish I am right next to, yet she can see them just as well. Plus, she occasionally keeps an eye on me, which is a nice additional safety element.

Wild-Goose Chase

I taught riflery at summer camp while I was growing up. I was an OK shot: I could always get five of five in the target, but only three of five in the black bull's-eye area. I could not see the bullet holes until I walked right up to the target, so I couldn't adjust and improve while shooting. However, I was very steady, getting the same scores standing and sitting as I did lying down, which confused some people. I focused a lot on safety.

As an adult, I once went goose hunting on Maryland's Eastern Shore. I was pretty amazed that I was able to get a hunting license, but no vision test was required.

It was very early when we left Baltimore for the Eastern Shore, where we arrived just before first light. We immediately put dozens of goose decoys out in the field next to our hunting blind. Many of the decoys were beautiful, some wood, some plastic, quite a few of them suitable for display on a fireplace mantel.

Others looked nice, but were just two dimensional. I was skeptical that the two-dimensional decoys would fool a goose.

We all got into the hunting blind, which was a narrow, half-underground shelter with a bench to sit on. This hiding place had a view of the field and the geese, but they cannot see you. Everyone sits in the hunting blind trying to attract the

big birds with goose calls. The top of the blind flips open when you want to stand up and shoot.

It was my turn. A whole big flock of geese landed among the decoys. The top of the blind was open, I stood up and aimed, but didn't shoot. Although I had thought that some of the decoys didn't look very convincing, as I aimed, I realized I couldn't tell the difference between the many geese on the ground and the many decoys.

The other hunters were yelling at me to shoot, but I still

couldn't see the difference between the real and fake geese. I held steady, not saying a word. The others kept shouting encouragement, some with much more than a touch of exasperation. The pressure was on. Someone else was going to take my shot if I didn't. I kept holding steady, still not saying a word. Finally, one goose took off from the ground and started to fly: clearly a real goose!

I shot it, and my family and I had it for Christmas dinner. It tasted great.

Close Shave at the Garden

Ice hockey: The New York Rangers were at home vs. the New York Islanders. It was late in the National Hockey League season, in New York City's magical world of Madison Square Garden. My friend John and I had good seats, just behind one of  the nets and just above the glass barrier surrounding the rink. It was an important, exciting, and sold-out game.

We hit the concession stands between the second and third periods, and switched seats when we got back to our row. Just as we were sitting down with our hot dogs and beer, a hard-shot line-drive puck was deflected just above the glass and came hurtling directly toward the guy sitting in front of John. The guy quickly ducked a tiny bit, raising his hands for protection. That move very slightly deflected the puck, so it was now heading right at John's head. He had just enough time for a little dodge and duck. The puck grazed his head, leaving a temporary crease but not drawing blood. It kept flying straight and fast, making a direct hit to the head of the man in the row behind us. That guy didn't have a chance: John had blocked his view until the very last split second. He was taken out of the game on a stretcher and did not return. John and the man in front of him were offered stretchers and medical attention, but each wanted to stay, have another beer, and watch the game.

If John and I had not unthinkingly switched seats, I would not have been able to see and dodge the puck in time—it would have been me hit in the head and taken out on a stretcher, rather than the fan in the row behind us. I haven't been to a hockey game since then. Next time, I'll know it's worth it to pay more to sit low and close enough to be behind the glass.

I only wear glasses when I'm playing tennis. After all, it is a noncontact sport.

Chapter 7

Smell, Taste, Hearing, Touch

> *"Observe, record, tabulate, communicate. Use your five senses. Learn to see, learn to hear, learn to feel, learn to smell, and know that by practice alone you can become expert."*
>
> *—William Osler*

Sense Your Way to a Better Brain

Brain scientists and doctors think that multiple pathways and types of input help learning, creativity, and memory. One way of doing this is to learn things via more than just one of our five senses. 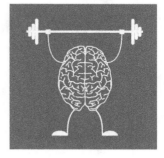 Not only is nonvisual learning worthwhile and fun, this challenge builds more synapses in the brain, making it stronger, more resilient, and less susceptible to deterioration later in life.

Sight is the primary sense, but if your sight is bad, you pay more attention to your other four. Those senses don't improve because your vision is bad, but if you rely on them more, pay attention to them more, and enjoy them more, you get better at using them.

Sense of Smell—Cooking

The late, great Julia Child—the terrific, celebrated star of *The French Chef* television series—observed that a good cook can

tell if a meal is done just by the smell. This is wonderful and practical news for people who have trouble reading meat and oven thermometers or judging by sight. Even when following a recipe, it is often unclear whether to take something off the heat a little sooner or let it cook an extra minute or two. Learning to rely on your sense of smell when cooking is fun and a good skill to have.

It can be tricky if a tiny drop spills onto a separate hot surface and gives off a competing—burning—smell, but that's no more confusing than competing messages from the other senses.

Sense of Smell—Safety

Pay attention to your sense of smell, it could save your life someday.

I lived in a studio apartment on the top floor of a five-story walk-up building on East 91st Street in New York City. I woke up one morning and noticed that I couldn't see the wall on the other side of my little apartment. Even though there

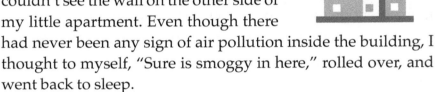

had never been any sign of air pollution inside the building, I thought to myself, "Sure is smoggy in here," rolled over, and went back to sleep.

What I saw wasn't smog—it was smoke, pouring into our homes from an abandoned building next door that had been torched. Had my nose been paying better attention, I might have been the first one out in the hall raising the alarm.

My next-door neighbor did the good deed of banging on everyone's door, yelling, "Fire!" I got dressed faster than any other time in my life and went out into the hall, just as a city firefighter came running up the stairs.

When you live on the fifth floor of a walk-up building, you get into pretty good shape just by coming home, plus you discover what kind of shape your visitors are in. Some people walk up and are OK with it, they might even think of it as a fun test. With some others, you could practically watch a whole movie before they pant their way to the top.

Not this firefighter. He was in boots, heavy uniform and helmet, oxygen tank on his back, and carrying an axe. While running up the stairs, he asked us in a completely calm, totally not-out-of-breath, friendly voice: "Could you guys give me a boost over the wall to the other building?"

We were happy to help, and followed him to the roof to provide the requested boost (he was heavy, in all that gear). Soon we heard him smashing a hole in the other building to let some of the fire's heat escape.

We looked over the back edge of our roof and could see the smoke pattern, as thick billows poured out of next door, made a U-turn, then streamed through our building.

Next we checked-out the front side of our building, where all the fire trucks and firefighters had gathered in the street below. The lead firefighter immediately used his bullhorn to yell up at us: "You idiots get off of the roof and out of the building!" We obeyed.

Knowing the firefighters were on the case and our building seemed safe, I stopped at my apartment on the way out, to take a shower and change my clothes.

Sense of Smell—Aroma Identification

If you ever get a chance to visit an aroma room at a wine store or winery, go for it. The one I went to in Napier, New Zealand, had 30 or so stations. At each station you would smell something that's used to describe a wine's taste (good or bad) and then guess what it is. Sometimes you would get an additional hint, perhaps a picture, before checking the answer.

The smells ran the gamut: flowers, fruits, beeswax, spices, vegetables, potting soil, petroleum, straw, and more. Sometimes I was sure I knew the scent, but I couldn't name it. After checking the answer, I would be surprised that I hadn't recognized it.

Trying to ID things just by smell is a fun self-test. The better you get at it, the more you will enjoy cooking, eating, and any accompanying wine.

Sense of Taste

Having poor vision just might improve your nonvisual memory. When I was a very little kid, my family lived near

the Pennsylvania Dutch country outside Philadelphia, so I grew to like the fabulous cheese made by the local Amish farmers. Then my family moved, and I forgot all about it. Twenty-five or so years later my ma bought some of that same cheese at her New York City neighborhood's farmers' market where some Amish farmers had a stand. She invited me over for lunch and without saying anything about a surprise taste test, she served some of the cheese. After a single bite I happily remarked that I loved and remembered the cheese but couldn't remember where I had it before. Not an A, but perhaps a pass.

Sense of Hearing — Safety, Movies, Language, Music

I love music but never listen on headphones or earbuds while walking, because I like to rely on my hearing to supplement

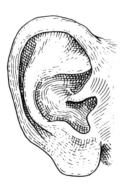

my vision. Every once in a while, hearing saves me from being hit by a car or truck. I try to make it a practice to look both ways before stepping off the curb, but feel much more comfortable crossing a street, going for a walk, or jogging if I am listening as well as looking.

Movie subtitles are difficult or impossible to read for people with bad eyes. On the other hand, dubbed translations in movies are great: We cannot see any differences between the way each character's mouth moves and the sound of the words coming out.

Those of us with poor eyesight may have an advantage

when learning to speak a foreign language. Poor vision makes us focus more on hearing, so we may be better at discerning dialects and pronouncing words with the right accents.

Playing trumpet

For musicians with bad vision it can be difficult or impossible to read sheet music, let alone sight-read. Rather than learning to play by a combination of reading music and by ear, some musicians rely more on learning strictly by ear, recognizing musical patterns, and memorizing passages of music, which is a super way to get better.

World-renowned figures who have gone this route include Andrea Bocelli, Mohan Chandrasekaran, Ray Charles, Sammy Davis Jr., José Feliciano, Terri Gibbs, Jeff Healey, Blind Willie Johnson, Ronnie Milsap, Ginny Owens, George Shearing, Diane

"Deedles" Schuur, Art Tatum, Nobuyuk Tsujii, Doc Watson, Edgar Winter, Johnny Winter, Stevie Wonder, and many others.

A minor still-very-long-way-to-go-example of this technique is me learning to play trumpet. If you are listening to the audio version of this book, that is me playing the musical background to part of this chapter.

In 2018 I participated in a Melbourne International Jazz Festival event called Jazz Massive. All musicians of any age or level were invited to an optional rehearsal. Afterward, hundreds of musicians gathered in the public square in front of the State Library of Victoria to play the music we had just seen and learned for the first time.

It was a nice day, so a good crowd turned out, as did TV cameras. I was among the six or eight trumpeters sharing one music stand and one set of sheet music. I could not see the sheet music without blocking everyone else's view, which I never want to do. Happily, my mate Travis Woods, a super trumpeter, led the trumpet section. I stood next to him and every once in a while, he let me know what key to play in, I improvised, and it all worked out well. Many other musicians have been just as helpful.

Hearing — Worth Two in the Bush

I had always avoided bird watch-ing. It struck me as a bit boring. Plus, I figured that poor eyesight would mean that I wouldn't spot most birds, and my lack of bird knowledge would practically guarantee I couldn't iden-tify the ones I did see. I assumed that I wouldn't be able to contribute.

Then my friend Rob invited my wife and I to join him and a group of his bird-watching friends as they surveyed Melbourne's Westgate Park. We wanted to see the park's naturally pink lakes, Rob has a lot of interesting friends, and we had never tried birding, so we went along. I also joined Rob for a bird survey of Melbourne's St. Vincent Gardens.

The bird watchers were an interesting and friendly group, very big on restoring and improving natural habitats for birds and other animals. They do regular surveys to track the avian population. I had expected them to identify bird types by their size, colors, markings, and calls, which they did. I was surprised and impressed that if that didn't narrow things down, many could also identify birds by flight pattern, which strikes me as pretty cool.

I surprised them a bit too, just by paying more attention to hearing. A few times I was the only one in the group who heard a bird rustling around in a tree or in some bushes. I couldn't see it, so I would point out the area to one of my more experienced companions, who despite good sight, usually couldn't see it either. We would watch for a bit and then most of the time a bird would fly or walk out, the birder would know what type it is, and count it in the survey. It was nice to be able to contribute.

Hearing vs. Sight — Be Nice

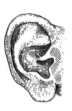 vs.

For some reason, people are nicer to people with poor vision than they are to people with poor hearing. We are very lucky. If you have bad eyesight, people are generally understanding, try to be helpful, don't get angry at you, and don't yell at you.

Sadly, people with poor hearing have a very different experience: Instead of speaking nicely in a louder voice, people often yell and get angry. It doesn't make sense, but it happens. No one gets to choose between the two, and no one likes to be yelled at. Be nice to everybody!

Sense of Touch—Holding Hands

Touch via holding hands is terrific for romance and for getting around, especially if it is so dark that it is difficult to see where you are going, or if one of your eyes sees better than the other. My left eye sees much better, so I especially like holding hands on the opposite side. With my wife, Judy, on my right, she covers what my bad eye might miss.

One time, Judy and I were walking with four friends along a very dark road near the Jersey shore. I could barely see anything, so reached over to hold hands with Judy, but she pushed my hand away. It's the only time that ever happened, so I was surprised, disappointed, and confused.

A few seconds later, after realizing what happened, it also turned out to be very embarrassing: It wasn't my wife Judy's hand. I had unknowingly reached out to the other Judy in our group, our wonderful actress friend Judy, who was with her future husband, Mark. I apologized.

It could have become a messy or awkward situation, or started a fight, but happily no one was annoyed, offended or angry. As often happens after an honest mistake, we all shared a good laugh.

On the Other Hand...

Sometimes I don't notice something because I don't see it, other times I don't notice something because I'm just not paying attention. People almost always give me the benefit of the doubt and think I didn't see it, which is nice.

There's more than one notorious example of me not paying attention, but my favorite happened when I was in junior high school. My ma and brother rearranged the furniture in the dining room, where we ate dinner together every evening. Months later, just as I was sitting down to eat, I commented that the new configuration was a great idea. I didn't understand why they thought my innocent observation was so hilarious, until they told me how much time had passed since they had made the change.

Cover blown.

What do you call a vegetable optometrist?
A see cucumber

What did the right eye say to the left eye?
Between you and me, there's something
that smells.

Chapter 8

Beauty, Relationships, Racial Harmony

"I am compelled to continuously see the bright side. It is in my DNA. … I feel joyful inside. I can't explain it."
—Goldie Hawn

Beauty

My cataract operations delivered a big, fast boost to my vision, improving it dramatically. Everyone I knew could still see much better than I could, but for me it was exciting and

fun. I spent time walking around just looking at everything with new eyes. Naturally, I shared this excitement with everyone, and everyone was happy for me.

After my first cataract operations, I told every woman I knew that with my improved vision I could now see that she was even more beautiful than I had thought. And told every guy I knew that he was a little uglier than I had thought. Of course, it wasn't true, but I said it to everyone as a human-nature experiment. Everyone. My ma, my brother, my relatives, my friends, neighbors, and people I worked with. All sizes, all shapes, all body types, all ages, all races, all heights, all weights.

Every single woman smiled, pretended to be embarrassed, thanked me, and believed me. Every single man looked down, gave a little embarrassed nod, and mumbled something about agreeing. Every single person agreed. It was so much fun, I did the same thing after my second cataract operation. I am probably lucky that some guy didn't kill me.

Don't Sweat the Details

The world is a beautiful place and it is even more beautiful if you have bad vision. Forests, mountains, meadows, cool buildings, modern and historical architectural marvels are very big and easy to see compared with smaller things like litter, power lines, graffiti, dirt, decay, light haze or smog. If you cannot see some of the small ugly stuff, the world looks better.

Drawing by Joan Brandt (Ken's ma)

As people get old, they might get a few streaks of grey, wrinkles, skin blotches, and some sagging. Some people have scars or other things. Luckily, the worse your vision, the less of this you notice. Everyone you know continues to look great. If your vision gets worse as they get older, this works out perfectly.

Everyone's home looks nicer to those of us with low vision. We have less ability to see dust and dirt, so if the home hasn't been cleaned well, we just don't notice.

This is great with other people's homes but can be a problem with our own. Resist the temptation to just ignore the whole subject and justify it by saying to yourself: I cannot see the dirt, so it cannot be too bad. I used to do that every once in a while, and by the time I noticed it, it could be really dirty.

Romance

One of the great things about romance is that it can involve a lot more than sight. When you are close to your loved one, you have the fun of soft touch, nice aroma, and sweet taste. Sharing with all the senses makes the romantic connection stronger and the relationship even more fun.

Poor vision enables you to be more considerate to anyone you sleep with. Because you have poor vision, you are used to walking around your home while seeing less. Without thinking about it, you have probably memorized the layout and are able to find your way easily in dim light or none at all. If my wife is asleep and I need to go to bed or get up in the dark, I don't have to turn the light on; I don't have to disturb her. I can be nice without even trying.

First Sight

Poor vision can make catching sight of lovers, friends, and associates more fun. If two people of equal vision approach each other from far away, they will likely see and then recognize each other at about the same time. Neither can tell if the other person was smiling all along or smiled because they recognized you. But if the two people have different vision levels, one of them gives and the other receives some happy feedback. The one who sees better will recognize the other person sooner, so will experience the joy of seeing the other person's face light up with a smile of recognition.

Friends

If you go to the movies or a concert, nearsighted people, such as me, like to sit up front. Farsighted people like to sit in the back. Everyone else, especially at movies, usually prefers somewhere in the middle. It is a very nice friend who will sit with you when you want to be close to the front or back. Cherish them.

Racial Harmony

Occasionally in high school or university I played in a shirts vs. skins pickup game of American football. As the name implies, the shirts team wears shirts, and the skins team doesn't. Sometimes this gets tricky because anyone, with any skin color, might be wearing a shirt that matches their skin. As a quarterback in

these games, I was an equal opportunity passer, invariably throwing a great pass to someone I thought was my receiver, and instead giving the other team an easy interception. It was best for me to play any other position in those games.

Poor-vision people can have difficulty differentiating people into groups, which could be a positive force for racial and ethnic harmony. People of any given ethnic group may have similar features and skin tone, but they vary within the group, and each group is similar to some other ethnic groups, which are always similar to some other ethnic group, etc., etc. There is overlap all over the world. The worse your eyesight, the more similar people look.

Summer tans blur differences even further. Anybody in any racial or ethnic group can have their hair whatever shade they want, including blues and greens. Same with tattoo inks. Lots of people are descended from multiple racial and ethnic groups. Human coloring, height, weight, features, all come in millions of different slight gradations.

For low-vision people, the details of this human spectrum are a bit of a blur. The goal of racial and ethnic tolerance and harmony may come easier to people who cannot always see the difference. There is a very good reason that justice is blind.

For several summers in high school I loved my job as a counselor at a multiethnic, multiracial camp. I was responsible for eight campers in a cabin. A brand-new batch of kids came in every two weeks, and I tried to memorize their names quickly. The vast majority of time, I could do this, no problem. However, once I had a cabin where I had trouble telling two of the kids apart. They weren't related, but were the same ethnic group, the same height, weight, and shape, had the same skin tone, haircut, and eye color. Their voices even sounded the same.

I didn't want anyone, especially them, to think I couldn't tell them apart. Simple solution—I spent two weeks pretending to mix up all eight of the campers' names, which confused and amused them, and united all of us as a team.

Bad eyesight can be a common bond between people of different races. No matter what race or ethnic group you are in, no matter what your nationality, religious beliefs, sexual orientation, age, or politics: If you have poor vision, you and I share some of the same challenges and hopefully enjoy some of the same anecdotes.

**A woman walks into an optician to return a pair of spectacles that she purchased for her husband a week before.
The assistant asks: What seems to be the problem?
The woman replies: I'm returning these spectacles I bought for my husband. He's still not seeing things my way.**

**I had to drive my girlfriend to the optometrist because she was having issues with her vision.
Turns out she was seeing other guys.**

**I think my optometrist is in love with me.
Every time I leave her office, she hands me a bottle of contact solution and says, "Eye care for you."**

I love my optometrist. She's a true visionary.

At a hotel restaurant, a man is sitting down to have dinner by himself, when he spots a woman sitting alone at the next table. Suddenly, she sneezes, and a glass eye comes flying straight out of her eye socket. In slow motion, *Matrix*-style, the man jumps up from the table and snatches it from the air. He then hands it back to her.

"This is so embarrassing," the woman says, and she pops her eye back in place. "I'm sorry to have disturbed you. Let me buy dinner to make it up to you. May I join you?"

The man nods. He enjoys the dinner because she is a stimulating conversationalist, has a great sense of humor, and they have a lot in common. He gets her phone number and asks, "You are the most charming woman I've ever encountered. Are you this nice to every guy you meet?"

"No," the woman replies. "You just happened to catch my eye."

Chapter 9

Mayhem, Curiosity, Mystery, Thief

> *"Life doesn't care about your vision. Stuff happens, and you've just got to deal with it. You roll with it; that's the beauty of it all."*
>
> —*Harold Ramis*

Photo Mayhem

Due to my crossed eyes, I often appear to be looking in the wrong direction in photos. Sometimes, just before the photographer snaps the photo, he or she asks me to look at the camera. Of course, I am already looking at the camera. It is great when the photographer asks me to look a little to the left or right, but that seldom happens.

Once at the wedding of two friends in upstate New York, the bride and groom invited me to be in some group photos. During the photo session, a member of the bride's family accused me of wrecking the wedding photos by crossing my eye. She was angry and doing her best to be protective of her relative on her big day, so I didn't see the point of explaining anything. I quickly apologized, and left the area.

Later, accompanied by the bride, the woman found me and apologized, which was very nice. It was clear that she felt terrible, which I felt bad about. A little after that the bride very nicely returned on her own to apologize for what happened and to thank me for handling everything so graciously, which was also very nice.

Getting kicked out of the unexciting photo session and instead going to the bar for some fine wine and interesting conversation, then getting two unexpected and heartfelt apologies made the wedding even more memorable and fun!

Curiosity and Suggestions

When two people with poor eyesight meet, they might not even realize the other one doesn't see well. If they both realize, they may share some of their experiences.

On the other hand, when people with good vision figure out that you cannot see very well, which usually takes about a second, a few of them ask a bunch of ridiculous, intrusive, impolite, or annoying questions. None of your answers will help them in their lives, but they just don't know any better, so they ask. This is especially likely to happen with kids and young adults.

They hold up a few fingers and ask you how many they are holding up. They tell you their vision and ask you what your vision is. They try on your glasses and are amazed that they cannot see well when wearing them. If you cannot see well enough to get a driver's license, they ask you about how you get around and how you feel about not being able to get to all the places they get to easily. Happily, as people grow up, they are less likely to ask such questions.

However, as people become adults, they become more likely to make a bunch of well-intentioned, but nevertheless annoying suggestions. If you wear glasses, they suggest you get contacts. If you wear contacts or have had a cataract operation, they suggest you get glasses. They suggest you use a trumpet lyre rather than holding the sheet music closer.

Thanks to these questions, suggestions, and sometimes accusations, you eventually develop a greater degree of tolerance and better social skills. After all, they are almost always based on bone-headed curiosity, misplaced sympathy, or a genuine desire to be helpful, rather than meanness. Dealing with these questions isn't fun or easy, but it does have an advantage. It forces you to develop a socially acceptable, polite, or humorous way to answer, change the subject, or walk away.

This is way better than the approach I took for a while when I was a little kid, which was to threaten or get into a fight with any little kid who had one of those questions or suggestions.

Speaking of a Few Fingers

For a while I had a regular full-time job all day, and also worked nights and weekends as a vendor in New York City's Madison Square Garden. I earned some extra money, plus I got to see the New York Rangers NHL hockey team and the New York Knicks NBA basketball team in action. Getting paid for showing up for work in the Garden was the closest I ever got to being a professional athlete.

At that time, you couldn't order food, beer, or soda delivered to your seat. You had to either get up to purchase it from the concession stands, or buy it from a vendor like me, who was wandering around selling stuff. I was over 18 so I could sell beer and didn't have to deal with ice cream or soda. "BEER HERE! COLD BEER!" That was me.

Beer was the most profitable thing to sell, but they wouldn't let you sell it before the national anthem. Instead you had to sell pretzels and popcorn to get everyone thirsty. Lots of salt. Toward the end of games you settled up: They tracked how much merchandise they gave you, you gave them the cash you received, and you would later get a check for 15 percent of the value of the pretzels, popcorn, and beer they supplied.

Some people would tip the vendors, especially if you kept coming back to them repeatedly with fresh beers. If you spilled anything, you bought it.

Vendors walk around all game, up and down a lot of steps, carrying trays of drinks and snacks, looking for people who want some of what they're offering, while yelling out, "POPCORN! PRETZELS! BEER HERE! BEER HERE!" It is a sweaty workout.

I really hustled, but I was an average vendor. Some people order things by raising their arm, standing up, and yelling to attract your attention—I could easily spot them, which was great. Others silently hold up a few fingers to indicate how many beers they want: I missed 99 percent of those customers.

You never know how well your vendor sees, so when you want to buy something, be nice, and make your order super obvious!

At one Knicks game, most of the vendors (including me) finished early, so I went back into the arena to watch the closing minutes of the game. I sat down in a very good empty courtside seat. A minute or two later a smiling guard in another section gestured for me to come with him. I smiled, waved him away, and kept watching the game. He came into my section, repeated his gesture, I again smiled, waved him away, and kept watching the game. Then he came right to my seat, quietly told me I had to get up right away and that he would explain why in a moment.

As we walked away together, he told me I had just sat right in front of the heads of the Knicks and Madison Square Garden. We didn't laugh too loudly until getting a little away from them, then watched the very end of the game together from the far end of the aisle.

On my first day as a vendor I had to buy a work apron, which has pockets for cash, and big, round orange buttons to pin to it for the things you are selling. I still have mine.

I worked as a vendor in the late 1970s, so the prices were much lower. My four buttons say: POPCORN & ICE CREAM 60 cents, PRETZELS 50 cents, SODA 65 cents, BEER $1.00. It is great for Halloween parties, where I often help the hosts serve things while practically yelling, "BEER HERE!" (or whatever I am helping to serve). Of course, I don't actually charge anyone.

Surprisingly, some people insist on tipping, which I thank them for and refuse. If they really insist, I take the tip, but then give it to the hosts, who are equally surprised.

A Sharing Mystery

When two people share a document, they usually put it half-way between them on a table or desk. This works fine, unless one needs to have it closer because of their vision. People are almost always willing to let you get closer to something if you explain that you cannot read it or see it.

I have been in this situation many times with many different people and the same thing always happens: I ask if it is OK to move it closer to me so that I can see it, they always say yes and move it. Then I always ask if the other person can still see it in the new position. The other person always happily says yes. So far, so good.

Then, slowly but surely, over and over, with many people in many different circumstances, the other person points to something or explains something or asks about something in the document. In the process they move it slightly closer to them and further away from me. After a while, the document is back in the middle, and I can no longer read it. If I once again ask if it is OK to move it closer to me, so I can see it, and I double-check to make sure they can see it after it is moved—the other person always laughs and happily agrees.

For some reason, some part of human nature, I don't know what or why, this loop will repeat indefinitely. Best to enjoy and wonder at human nature, laugh internally, keep repeating the loop, and/or try to speed-read and memorize the document's key points when it is close to you and then let it go.

Menu Mystery

Reading a restaurant menu isn't always a piece of cake. Handheld versions often have small print, hard-to-read fonts, or low-contrast color combinations. Menus posted on the wall, behind the counter, or on boards may be too far away to read. Some are crafted in beautiful but indecipherable script. Dark restaurants may offer great atmosphere, but they're not necessarily reader friendly. It can be uncomfortable explaining that you cannot see the menu, pulling out a magnifying glass, or using your mobile phone's light or an app, but at least one or two other options are usually available.

Option 1 – Order something they are likely to have. Just take a guess. Base your guess on the time of day and type of restaurant. For breakfast, eggs are standard in many countries. For lunch or dinner, burgers in America, chicken parma in Australia, plain or cheese in a pizza place, pho in a Vietnamese restaurant, or pad Thai in a Thai restaurant, to scratch the surface. If they don't have it, ask what alternatives they offer. The same thing works for drinks: Coke, milkshake, the house red, the local beer. If your favorite type of wine or brand of soda or beer is popular, many restaurants are likely to carry it.

Option 2 – Go social! Servers or waitstaff usually welcome friendly questions about the food on offer. What are the most popular dishes? Which do you recommend? Which are your favorites? Which ones have the biggest or smallest portions?

Wine lists are sometimes even harder to read than menus, so win over the waiter or sommelier by asking which wine would go best with your dish. If you're feeling adventurous, the answers to these questions could tempt you into discovering delicious new favorites.

People are almost always happy to answer one or two questions, which can lead to a fun little conversation. You don't need to be able to see the menu or mention that you cannot see the menu.

Catching a Thief

I've shared a lot of adventures with my friend John ever since we met and got into a fight in second grade. We each think we won. Some adventures were planned, like spelunking. Others just happened.

Take a certain weeknight in the 1980s, when John and I went out for a few drinks after work. We both had to be at the office the next day, but having beers is fun, New York City is fun, and we hoped to meet some women.

After many hours at the bar and no success meeting women,

we headed back toward John's car and my apartment, both near East 91st Street and Third Avenue in Manhattan.

We were walking up Third Avenue when John suddenly broke into a run. I had no idea why he was running, but we have been best mates since second grade, so naturally I trust him. Without either of us saying a word, I took off with him.

I glanced behind me: No one appeared to be chasing us. But as we got closer to John's car, I saw what he saw: Someone had broken into his grey 1979 Buick LaSabre, and was robbing him. We were not being chased: We were trying to catch a thief!

John and I ran as fast as we could. We were in our 30s then, and not as quick as we were when we were on the same track and cross-country teams in high school. In those days, he was a much better runner than me, but by the '80s we were about the same, and occasionally took part in NYC Road Runners races. However, we weren't nearly as speedy as we could have been if we had on running gear, rather than business suits and dress shoes, and hadn't spent most of the night drinking.

We chased the thief as he fled west on East 91st Street's sidewalk. Then he ducked into the middle of the street, with John ducking right behind him. I kept running on the sidewalk, and was now parallel with the robber.

It was way past midnight, and there were plenty of dark areas between the streetlamps. As we neared the end of the block at Lexington Avenue, I kept glancing in the direction of the bandit and failed to notice a mattress someone had thrown out, in an unlit spot in the middle of the sidewalk.

I tripped over the mattress but there was no cushy landing. I had way too much momentum. I was in the air long enough to realize that I would go way beyond the mattress and smash into some garbage cans and the pavement. I knew the whole thing would probably hurt.

I was right. After knocking over the garbage cans with my landing and getting some minor bruises and scrapes, I saw the thief and John turn uptown on Lexington Avenue. I started following them, though I had dropped farther behind, thanks to my mattress misadventure. I saw them turn east somewhere, but I wasn't sure at which intersection. I kept sprinting up Lexington, looking down each block, hoping to spot them. No luck. I eventually turned on 96th Street and started running east.

At that point the police showed up. They pulled me over, put me up against their car, and frisked me, thinking I was the culprit. I was too out of breath to explain. But they soon let me go, without saying why or telling me what they had just heard over their car radio.

So, I decided to retrace my steps and run down Lexington, in case the thief had circled around. I headed south almost to the corner of 92nd Street, where I spotted the robber surrounded by a circle of people. I sprinted up to them and jumped over the crowd toward the bad guy.

It was a very good jump. My waist was at shoulder-height of the people I leapt over. Again, I had a lot of momentum. However, at the height of my jump I noticed something that would have been good to know before liftoff: Everyone in the circle was a cop, with their batons and guns at the ready.

Luckily John, whom I hadn't seen either, jumped up to say I was with him. He had been so out of breath from the chase that he hadn't been able to explain anything to the police. His first non-out-of-breath words were to save me from the authorities, which was very nice of him.

My friend later updated me about what happened after I lost sight of them. As he pursued the thief east on 93rd Street, John yelled at everyone he passed to call the cops. A bicycle rider joined in the yelling and the chase. They zigzagged around a bit to Second Avenue, where they went north, then south until John caught the guy.

However, my friend was too exhausted to hold on to the thief; he got away and the pursuit resumed, this time heading in the opposite direction. John and the bicycle rider continued yell-

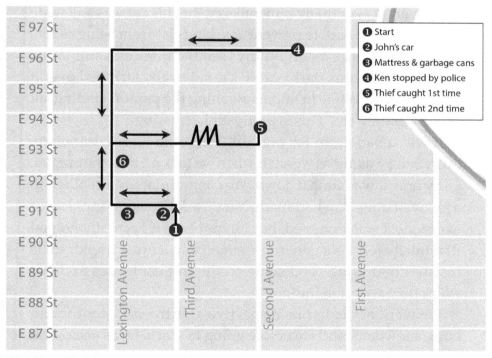

Thief Chase Map

ing "Call the police," to everyone they passed. A doorman saw the robber toss a gym bag full of stuff behind some bushes and reported it to the cops. The bag turned out to contain burglary tools and John's car radio.

John and the bicycle guy chased the thief back to Lexington and almost to the corner of 92nd Street, where my friend caught him for the second time, and this time was able to hold on until the law arrived.

When the police swooped in, the thief was so nervous that he threw up on several of them. The helpful bike rider took off once he saw that the robber had been caught.

That wasn't the end of our adventures that evening.

John and I eventually remembered that his car was still wide open, so we ran back to prevent anything else from being stolen. In my hurry, once again I didn't see the mattress, still in the middle of the same dark part of the sidewalk. I tripped over it a second time. While in midair awaiting the painful landing, all I could think was, "This is pretty embarrassing."

It was a bad night for my suit. We got to John's car, where everything was just as we left it when we took off after the burglar.

By now it was almost dawn. We congratulated each other on a job well done: We had made New York City a safer place for everyone. I was involved, but I'm not sure if I actually helped that much. John is a generous person and a great friend, so he insisted that I deserved some credit and continues to do so every time we retell the story.

We went home to our respective apartments, slept for an hour, showered, and ate before going to work. I was useless on the job that next day, so I spent most of my time telling the story to my fellow consultants and to clients. John did the same with his work colleagues.

We found out later that the thief's fingerprints were on record from several unsolved robberies. His burglary tools were found as evidence, and he was caught in the act of breaking into and robbing John's car, so he pleaded guilty and went to jail. Neither John nor I nor the doorman who saw him try to hide his burglary tools had to testify, and it didn't matter that the mysterious but helpful bicycle rider disappeared.

John even got back the stolen car radio from the police, once they finished the investigation.

Solving the murder of the eye doctor was difficult... but the cops managed to close the lid on it.

What was the glasses' lens's excuse to the policeman? I've been framed.

Did you hear about the optometrist who helps police solve crimes? He's a private eye.

Chapter 10
Final Thoughts

> *"Just because a man lacks the use of his eyes doesn't mean he lacks vision."*
>
> *—Stevie Wonder*

See the Bright Side

Everyone with poor eyesight must be a bit adventurous to do some of the same things routinely done by people with normal eyesight. If you are not there yet, you might be in the future: Many people's vision deteriorates a bit as they age, pushing them into this adventure zone.

Clearly good sight is better than bad sight, however, in my experience, there are some positives to having poor vision.

For me, a longer life, more adventure and discovery, and greater creativity and imagination are the bright side of poor vision. I believe my bad eyesight has contributed to better hand-eye coordination, balance, presentation skills, and enhanced use of my other senses. Poor vision also makes it easier to enjoy a more beautiful world and improve racial harmony. Seeing the bright side makes life more fun for you and those around you.

Once you've done everything you can to protect your eyes, take care of your eye health, and safely improve your vision, then:

- Relax and be grateful for whatever sight you have;

- When you decide to go for something, give it a red-hot go, and

- Love the challenges, see the bright side, appreciate the advantages, and enjoy the adventures of poor eyesight.

Why I Wrote this Book Now

Growing up, I was not comfortable discussing challenges I faced with people of normal vision. They might realize that my vision is worse than they thought, feel sorry for me, or treat me differently. Instead, I found it worked for me to just silently fight any fears and enjoy my everyday adventures.

Another reason I avoided discussing the subject of poor vision until now is that I thought it might be detrimental to my career and job prospects, and I didn't want anyone feeling sorry for me, or trying to help with things that I don't need assistance with. Now I am retired, so I don't care about my career. Plus, I hope this book will help and amuse people with poor eyesight and their friends and families.

Hey, You… Yes, You!

I am a little worried that some of my friends will read this book, learn that I have much worse vision than they realized, and change their attitude toward me. Sadly, this happened a bit with a few people who read drafts of the book as I was writing it. I hope that old and new friends who read this book will continue to ignore everything about my vision and treat me the same way as they always have (good and bad!).

An Invitation!

Do you have poor eyesight? Would you like to share some stories or tips with the world? I am assembling them into a collection for a future book, and it would be great to include your suggestions and experiences. Adventures, advantages, anecdotes, humor, quotes, tips, and/or jokes are all welcome. Use the contact form on my website: www.kenbrandt.com. Hope to hear from you!

An ophthalmologist, an optometrist, and an optician walk into a bar...

Nobody could see the difference.

About the Author

Ken does his best – some days are way better than others – to live by his three favorite quotes. This is the second of them:

"The full measure of a man is not to be found in the man himself, but in the colors and textures that come alive in others because of him."

–Albert Schweitzer

Ken Brandt has had poor vision and slightly crossed eyes since birth. He has had six eye operations (including detached retina and cataract operations in both eyes) and was legally blind for parts of his life.

Despite (or perhaps in part because of!) his bad eyesight, Ken seems to have discovered the recipe for joyful living early on. As revealed in this book, his vision doesn't interfere with his positive outlook, sense of adventure, and ability to find humor in almost every situation.

On both the business and personal sides, Ken's life has been enriched by travel, friendship, and a knack for finding creative solutions to knotty problems.

During more than three decades in the corporate world, Ken held senior management and management consulting positions in information technology and information security, earning numerous certifications.

Ken still has his very first pair of glasses!

Ken worked with a variety of multinational companies, infrastructure firms, and government agencies in North America, Europe, Asia, and Australia. An entertaining speaker, Ken has lectured on an array of topics at universities, associations, and in corporate settings.

Ken has effectively applied his business experience as a volunteer director on the board of several nonprofits, including information security- and music-related organizations.

Since retiring, Ken maintains a busy and varied schedule, focusing on writing, including this book. He makes time to pursue his lifelong enthusiasm for sports and fitness, and is an avid amateur New Orleans-style jazz trumpeter. He continues to accept speaking engagements.

Ken and his wife, Judy Roberts Brandt, have been married for more than 20 years. The two spent most of their lives in New York City, and now live in Melbourne, Australia.

More details:

- Learn about Ken's vision history, use of glasses, contact lenses, eye patches, and eye operations, in Chapter 2, Science to the Rescue.
- For stories about Ken's bad eyesight-related adventures and life hacks, see most other chapters!
- Take a deeper look at Ken's professional background at: https://au.linkedin.com/in/kenbrandt2

**My optometrist told me I have bad vision...
I don't see the problem.**

Dedication

"All that I am, or hope to be, I owe to my mother."
–Abraham Lincoln

This book is dedicated to my parents, Joan Walsh Brandt and Carl Patteson (Pat) Brandt. They are/were great parents. My father had good vision; my ma had good vision most of her life, but now has poor vision. My father died when I was 10. After that, my ma raised Peter (great brother, good vision) and me on her own. She has been giving us useful advice and leading by example our whole lives, so the lion's share of this dedication goes to my ma. I hope she finds this book humorous and helpful.

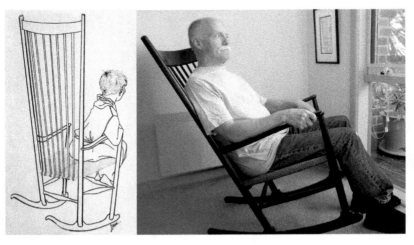

**Younger, and 57 or so years later. Drawing by Joan Brandt (Ken's ma).
Drawing and rocker are wonderful gifts from Joan Brandt.**

Of the book's jokes, this is my ma's favorite:

A green snake goes to the optometrist because his eyesight is failing.

"It's actually affecting my life.
I can't hunt anymore because I can't see."

The doctor fits the snake for glasses and the snake immediately notices an improvement in his eyesight.

A week later, the doctor calls the snake to check on how the glasses are holding up.

"They're fine," the snake answers. "But now I'm being treated for depression."

"Depression?" the doctor asks.

"Yeah, my eyesight cleared up, but it made me realize I've been dating a garden hose."

Philanthropy

"Remember that the happiest people are not those getting more, but those giving more."
–H. Jackson Brown Jr.

Thank you for buying this book. Your purchase has helped two great vision causes: I am donating 10 percent of my book royalties (5 percent each) to:

- Massachusetts Eye and Ear, for eye research, and

- The Fred Hollows Foundation, for ending avoidable blindness.

Massachusetts Eye and Ear is the flagship research and teaching hospital of the Department of Ophthalmology at Harvard Medical School. It unites researchers from three historical institutions. Their investigators conduct cross-institutional eye research in a dozen laboratories, institutes, and centers of excellence. I had both of my detached retina operations at Massachusetts Eye and Ear. Each saved my vision.

The Fred Hollows Foundation is a charity that works to restore sight to people who are needlessly blind. The Foundation provides affordable eye health-care services to those who need it most in Australia and 25 other countries around the world. So far, they've been able to restore sight to more than 2 million people. But there is still much to be done. Right now there are 36 million people in the world who are blind – 4 out 5 don't need to be.

An unexpected donation was made to a school for low-vision and blind children. During the thank-you celebration and reception, the school's principal told the donor: "Wow, they didn't see that coming!"

Acknowledgements

"Feeling gratitude and not expressing it is like wrapping a present and not giving it."
—William Arthur Ward

Thank you to my wife, Judy Roberts Brandt, who created the snappy book covers, easy-to-read book design, and most of the photographs. See: judybrandtdesign.com

Thank you to Cheyney State Teachers College (now Cheyney University of Pennsylvania), which had a great, fun prekindergarten program for kids with bad vision. Special thanks to my teacher Ruth MacIntosh. I loved being in that program and am a happy and grateful alumnus.

Thank you to the medical professionals who enabled me to see: the doctors and nurses at Magee Hospital (Pittsburgh, Pennsylvania, USA) where I was born (now UPMC Magee-Womens Hospital); eye doctors Rob McDonald (Philadelphia, Pennsylvania, USA); Ichiro Okamura (Boston, Massachusetts, USA); Albert Ackerman, Harvey Topilow, and Robert Cykiert

(New York, New York, USA); Daniel Chiu and Mark Troski (Melbourne, Australia).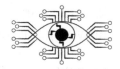

Thank you to my wife, brother, ma, and friends who read drafts of this book and suggested great improvements: Judy Roberts Brandt (twice!), Peter Brandt (twice!), Joan Walsh Brandt, Wendy Enevoldsen, Paul Kastner, Julie Maguire, Pete Paisley, Deb Saltzman (twice!), Mark Sanders, John Schofield (aka Jay Schofield), Cass Treagus, Mike Trovato,

Russell D. Vines, and Rob Youl (four times!). **Thank you** to Andrew Moffat for his assistance with the Menu Mystery section.

While writing this book, I had the chance to read excerpts aloud and talk about parts of the book to groups that provided helpful feedback. **Thank you** to everyone in these groups: the Melbourne Write Club meetup, Melbourne Writers Social meetup, and South Melbourne Toastmasters (especially Tess Binns).

Thank you to my nephew Tyler Brandt, who converted a tough-to-understand table of eyesight figures and events into Chapter 2's snappy multinational line graph.

Thank you to everyone who helped brainstorm book ideas: Jake Brandt, Larry Budde, Mike Krutsch, Morgan Paisley, Tina Smith, Andrea Sprirov, Belinda Weaver, many of the people mentioned in the

book, and many of the people thanked elsewhere in the Acknowledgements.

Thank you to my friends Matt Pini and Con Sweeney, for their valuable insights and suggestions about intellectual property and book marketing, respectively.

Thank you to my friend and editor Elzy Kolb, whose talent, good humor, and hard work made this book much better than it would have been without her.

Thank you to my friend Rob Youl for writing and narrating the fabulous Foreword.

Four friends added their wonderful voices, talents, joy, and enthusiasm to the audio version of this book. **Thank you** to Rob Youl for speaking his foreword, Joyce Agee for speaking the quotes; actor Gil Tucker for speaking the jokes; and James McGowan for friendly and knowledgeable audio guidance, use of his professional audio equipment, and engineering the audio book.

Recording with Joyce (left) and James (center).

Recording with Gil (right).

Last, but not least, **thank you** to everyone who was happy to be mentioned in the book.

A collection of corny eyesight jokes wouldn't be complete without a few knock-knock jokes. Here are two, and they are dedicated to everyone mentioned in this book.

>**Knock knock**
>**Who's there?**
>**Eye...**
>**Eye who?**
>**Eye got one more knock-knock joke for you!**
>
>**Knock knock**
>**Who's there?**
>**Eyeball...**
>**Eyeball who?**
>**Eyeball my eyes out every time you go!**

Appendix

Understanding the Eye Chart

> *I do my best – some days are way better than others – to live by my three favorite quotes. This is the third of them.*
>
> *"Every morning in Africa, a gazelle wakes up. It knows that it must run faster than the fastest lion or it will be killed. Every morning a lion wakes up. It knows that it must outrun the slowest gazelle or it will starve to death. It doesn't matter whether you are a lion or a gazelle: when the sun comes up, you'd better be running."*
>
> *–The Economist*

This appendix explains the Ken's Corrected Eyesight chart, which appears at the start of Chapter 2. I have greatly benefited from corrected vision all my life: correction with eyeglasses at first, followed by contact lenses, and then the artificial lenses implanted during cataract operations.

20/20 means that the eye sees at 20 feet what a normal-sighted person's eye sees at 20 feet; 6/6 is the metric equivalent of 20/20. Six meters = roughly 20 feet. 20/200 means that the eye sees at 20 feet what a normal-sighted person's eye sees at 200 feet; 6/60 is the metric equivalent of 20/200.

The definition of legally blind varies depending on the country and government agency. Generally, a person is considered legally blind if their better eye's corrected vision is 20/200 (6/60) or worse.

For me, "20/410 or lower" on the chart means three measurements of 20/800 (6/240) and one of 20/1,200 (6/360). The three vertical lines indicate three of my six eye operations.

Information on my eyesight prior to 1968 is based on my ma's notes. Thanks, Ma! Information on my eyesight from May 1982 onward is based on my eye doctors' records. Thanks, Docs! Unfortunately, I was not able to obtain any of my 1954-1981 eye doctors' records, nor half of my 1982-2006 eye doctors' records.

Eye Doctor: Read the bottom line of the eye chart...
Patient: Copyright 1997

CPSIA information can be obtained
at www.ICGtesting.com
Printed in the USA
LVHW060948241020
669275LV00056B/1260/J